THOU SHALT NOT STEAL

And Other Myths and Shenanigans of the Business World

Ray Knudson

PAGE PUBLISHING, INC.
Conneaut Lake, PA

First originally published by Page Publishing 2020

ISBN 978-1-6624-0743-7 (pbk)
ISBN 978-1-6624-0744-4 (digital)

Printed in the United States of America

CONTENTS

ACKNOWLEDGMENTS

There are many people that I am greatly indebted to and mention just a few here publicly.

Mike and Bill Gibbons ran a very successful construction company that performed work throughout the western states, and this was in addition to providing me and my family with food, shelter, and clothing for many years. They are both gentlemen in every sense of the word.

My mother who has encouraged me and been my cheerleader in everything that I have ever done. My successes were expected, and my failures were obviously the fault of others.

My wife, Karin, has that German loyalty gene and apparently believes that you live with your mistakes. She has put up with my foolishness for more years than anyone should have to. She is beautiful and smart thus offsetting my weaknesses and shortcomings.

And lastly, my son, Mike, who is an author in his own right. His critique, suggestions, and comments have contributed greatly to whatever success this book might achieve.

For Karin

INTRODUCTION

This book began as a personal history of my business endeavors, experiences, and accomplishments, but somehow this got sidetracked. The interesting characters, incidents, and situations that I witnessed along the way completely overshadowed my original intent. These schemes and shenanigans make for a much more interesting and entertaining read as well as a somewhat larger book.

Let me begin by saying that this book is not a business tome on the sins of Madoff, or the ENRON fraud, or Kozlowski's TYCO, or any of the others of similar ilk. The key players in these were already wealthy and successful men who through arrogance and greed apparently lost track of reality. Their escapades and the almost-unfathomable scale of monies and hubris involved are the basis for many books that have been and are yet to be written.

This book is about the employees on lower rungs of the corporate ladder. And particularly those who found access to the company cookie jar through very little effort, or ingenuity on their part.

These were folks that were hired with no thoughts or intentions other than to be good employees. They were then placed into positions where, due to lax rules and few safeguards, the lid to the company cookie jar was all but open and access almost too easy to resist.

I would like to make known up front that I am writing this book as an observer of these deeds as opposed to that of a participant. I certainly have done my share of pilfering the typical office supplies and maybe fudged a bit in other areas but certainly not any more than that which, if not deemed acceptable, is overlooked. I use the term "as I recall" a few times, and to the best of my recollection, I believe reflect fairly accurate accounts of the events mentioned.

There are similar activities to those examples outlined in the book that are probably ongoing. The schemes and methods being so simple that those involved have yet to be found out. Those that are caught with their hand in the company cookie jar usually became so greedy that they passed the point of reasonability and that was the cause of the demise of most of the schemes. It seems that larceny exists at both ends of the spectrum and all areas in between.

There are many of the incidents herein that are known to me firsthand. Many perpetrators would be considered my friends at one time and some probably still are. They were put into positions, through no fault of their own, where there were very little controls between them and the company cookie jar. I will try to explain as best I can the events and shortcomings leading up and through the conclusion of each of these events.

Most of us try to observe the thou–shalt–not–steal ethic regardless of what religion we profess to be, or if we are not religious, it is either a written or unwritten law of all societies that I am aware of. Whoever it was that professed "I can resist anything but temptation" nailed it pretty well. I believe that many of us have a threshold at which it would not be wise to be tempted especially when the odds of being found out are between slim and none.

I put forth this book not to criticize the thief as he has already suffered the pain and humiliation of being found out, and in many cases, restitution has been made. And I do not encourage the behavior that led to the offense but put it forth maybe as a restraint or lesson that could be learned by both a tentative crook, or a company official in charge of setting up the necessary procedures, or lack thereof that enable a company to be compromised.

I pass on my observations, experiences, and thoughts as they pertain to the subject as well as other random and disjointed musings that might, I would hope, be enlightening, entertaining or, by some stretch of the imagination, have some redeeming quality.

I have had a variety of jobs during my lifetime from summer jobs during school that included construction, restaurants, service stations, farming, and a short time in government work that included a stint in the Army, a short time at the IRS, and a short time as a postal employee. My longest period of employment was for a large construction company at which I held various positions ranging from laborer, accounting clerk to data processing manager. I am currently and have been a real estate appraiser for the last few years. Somehow this work slowed down considerably for a time, and I have included a chapter regarding this.

The construction industry remains my favorite. The people in this industry are the most diverse, independent, hardheaded, outrageous, and colorful characters as there are in any industry, but that is a subject for another time.

CHAPTER ONE

Think Twice Before You Steal:
It Can Be Addicting

The difference between most of us and those behind bars is that they got caught and we did not. That is a pretty general observation as some of us at various times have compromised the system in some fashion or other, and we may not have been behind bars; however, had we been caught, our lives might have been very different.

I would hope that this book might result in someone maybe thinking twice before succumbing to temptation that is at their threshold of "do I" or "don't I." I would also hope that employers have the necessary policies, procedures, and controls in force between the company cookie jar and the employees that make it somewhat difficult to get a hand into.

We are not talking about the dedicated criminal who will compromise the system regardless of the measures that have been taken. This is about the individual who, through no fault of their own, finds the company wallet open and the contents there for the taking.

I find that in the majority of instances that the employee is seldom found out on the first venture. It is only after the thefts become more frequent and the amounts greater that carelessness appears to set in, and the scheme is found out. The penalty, when discovered, is also quantified with each additional theft. Those employees that are caught on their first attempt may or may not be prosecuted or even fired, but after a long pattern of thefts, there is little sympathy for the person, or the deed.

There are cases and examples included of theft, embezzlement, pilfering, or whatever the current politically correct name for stealing is. I have known many of the individuals involved personally, and in some cases, I have sympathy for them and in others probably not. Their lives were all changed considerably. In many cases, repayment was made by liquidating whatever they had accumulated through their lives as well as help from their family members and friends. Their future prospects for employment were sharply curtailed, and in some cases, prison time was necessary. The spouse, children, family, and friends were embarrassed and humiliated.

I will begin with some comments and a few observations of the old-time mom-and-pop stores. They were around during a much simpler time and have long since disappeared from the landscape. Whether they were set up purposely or by accident, they were by design a secure environment that continues to be envied to this day.

CHAPTER TWO

Mom-and-Pop Industries: Now There Was a Secure Cookie Jar

The mom-and-pop industries of yesteryear had a method of keeping the old cookie jar lid pretty secure, and even today, we are trying to replicate, emulate, and duplicate it on a much larger scale, and it is proving very difficult. Most mom-and-pop operations have long since been eradicated by the entry of the large chains of grocery stores, restaurants, gas stations, and so on.

When we drive through older residential neighbor-hoods, we often see the occasional out-of-place building that has very little character, probably rectangular shaped with flat roof and large front windows. These are usually the remnants of and about all that are left of the old neigh-borhood grocery stores that have long since been converted to residences or rental units.

The old mom-and-pop stores received their names as that was exactly what they were. The employees and the owners were mom and pop. The old grocery store had a front entrance with a small door, and there was probably also a back door that remained locked except when receiv-ing deliveries. The cash register would reside next to the front door. Mom would run the cash register and greet and check the customers as they came and went from the prem-ises while Pop would keep the shelves stocked and carry out bags as needed.

There were other variations of the mom-and-pop stores, one of which was the mom-and-pop restaurant. Again, basically the same setup as the grocery store. Mom or Dad would man the cash register also located next to the front door to take the money and greet (check out) the customers. While the other would be in the back cooking with probably one or more of the kids, or other relatives waiting on tables. Again, the person at the cash register would be the only one handling the money. Customers would receive their bill at the table and then proceed to the cash register that was conveniently located on the only way out to pay the bill.

The old mom-and-pop grocery stores were just that—grocery stores. They did not sell hardware, clothing, fast foods, or such. However, the hardware and clothing stores of the era were also variations and knockoffs of the old mom-and-pop stores.

Mom and pop also ushered in the credit era by allowing families to charge their groceries and paying for them on payday. This created two things: a loyal clientele as well as keeping products moving out the door every day in an orderly manner rather than having big runs on payday. There was no interest, or carrying charges added to the account, and whatever expenses that may have occurred due to the occasional deadbeat customers were probably included in the markup of the goods.

This also created the spin-off of another cottage industry whereby the store proprietor, in some cases, became a sort of private banking system making loans to their customers for needs other than groceries. The track record that the customer had built up by paying off their grocery bills created a credit history upon which a loan amount and interest rate would be based and in these transactions interest was charged to the borrower.

These were the forerunners of the businesses of today in which the credit departments contribute in some cases almost as much to the bottom line as that of the products and services that are sold.

The mom-and-pop stores were laid out in such a manner that there were very few additional controls that were necessary. There was usually only one entrance open at any time, and it was always monitored by one person who handled the money and that person usually had an ownership interest in the success of the business.

Times were simple, and whether the stores were set up with a layout conducive to security was accidental or intentional, the design worked very well.

Compare a restaurant of today with the old mom-and-pop establishment. Servers of today are at the low end of the food chain, especially in smaller restaurants. They are the ones that take the money or credit card and, in some cases, actually have access to the till and make the change or charge the credit card. Tips are their main source of income as wages are usually negligible, and there is no ownership incentive to be careful (honest).

This is not to say that there were not any compromises in the old mom-and-pop operations, but to whatever extent, there was a compromise, in most cases, it remained in the family.

There is also another reason put forth by those who lived and remember the good old days of mom-and-pop stores. Their contention is that there were fewer problems in the good old days with shoplifting, stealing, and other crimes because there was a much better grade of people, more honest, and upright than our current population. We did not lock our doors, keys were left in the car, and Sundays would find most everyone in church.

This appears to be a somewhat selective memory problem that oldsters seem to have when remembering the good old days. I believe that police and sheriff departments as well as jails, courts, prisons, and penitentiaries are not a new phenomenon. They have been with us since about the beginning of time. I believe that it was no accident that this system and the security that it provided was set up to monitor the patrons of the time. It was designed to keep the honest folks honest as well as those with a less-than-trustworthy nature.

CHAPTER THREE

The New Cookie Jar Is Much More Difficult
to Protect from Being Compromised

Mom and Pop certainly had a relatively easy time of keeping their business assets secure. But the times have changed,
and access to the company cookie jars of today are many
and diverse. While they are being drained by payrolls and
other expenditures including materials, supplies, equipment, rentals, advertising, donations, fees, subcontractors,
legal services, outside auditors, etc. They are hopefully

being filled with revenues from contracts, subcontracts, product sales, services, and other income as well as lines of credit from banks to cover expenses and expansion needs when there is insufficient revenue.

Each step is governed by policies and procedures and other safeguards and assurances that hopefully allow only legitimate expenses to be paid and to insure that all the income is received.

I am always impressed by the large franchises and nationwide stores that are able to set up the necessary and effective policies, procedures, and controls that keep them secure and successful. Continued diligence is a necessary and ongoing and never-ending job as each new development for increased productivity and efficiency comes along they bring a new set of challenges with them and needs for new safeguards and procedures to prevent them for being compromised.

Mom and Pop did not have to worry about unpaid items going out the front door in backpacks and computer bags. They did not worry about employees stealing items out the back door by placing items in dumpsters, or the like to be picked up after work. Now we have devices that must be removed with a special tool at the cash register, or else, an alarm will be sounded if they leave the store. Surveillance cameras are now placed throughout the stores in hopes of catching, or at least slowing down this pilferage.

Checks are now electronically signed and mailed with very little human intervention. Bank accounts are now accessed directly. Credit and debit cards are used to compromise the system.

It is an ongoing contest between the new technologies that come along to increase our efficiency and productivity and those trying to compromise them for their own personal gain. Each new technology requires a new set of policies and procedures and safeguards.

The next few chapters, we examine actual examples of what can happen when there is a lack of safeguards and controls, causing a somewhat loose lid on the company cookie jar.

CHAPTER FOUR

A Volunteer Position in a Charity that Deals
in Cash Needs a Person of Strong Principles
as well as Strong Financial Controls in Place

One of my first jobs was at the local post office. I hired on
as a temporary employee and did not hang around long
enough to become a permanent. This was the first time
that I had worked with coworkers who were supposedly
grown-up adults, and this was, in most cases, their lifetime occupations. I certainly had my eyes opened as I was

expecting something more than I got. It wasn't long before I realized that adults are just older kids with all the problems, pettiness, jealousies, and insecurities of teenagers.

My job was to substitute for letter carriers and clerks on their days off. In this position, I had to learn each of their routes and duties. The full-time carriers usually lived within the boundaries of their routes. This was convenient as most routes on most days could be completed in somewhat less than the time allotted. I assumed that they spent their free time at their home and then would finish their jobs and return to the post office at the proper time.

They made it clear to me that I was not to return early as it would make them look bad. I got fairly proficient at goofing off at coffee shops, service stations, or other places killing time until it was okay to return. This seemed odd to me at first; however, I soon fell in line, adjusted my time, and enjoyed the work.

This was also my first experience with a union. The workers all belonged to a postal union. I attended one union meeting at which a national union representative was present. I listened with amazement while each of my full-time coworkers complained, in some cases to the point of tears, about the terrible conditions in which their work subjected them to including their supervisors, long hours, and the length of their routes. All this was new to me as I worked beside them each day, and they certainly appeared to enjoy their work

This was an eye-opener to me at that time; however, as I look back, it appears to be a fairly typical attitude that appears to permeate most industries. I like to use the analogy that most workers are similar to farmers of which I know a few, and as long as a farmer is complaining things are usually all right, it is when they no longer complain that there are usually problems. I will address other union experiences later in the book.

Now I will get to the meat of the case. The period in which this took place was some years ago. It was at the time when my bosses, the postmaster, and assistant postmaster served at the pleasure of whichever political party was in power. The postmaster and assistant postmaster each belonged to a different political party. The postmaster position was subject to political patronage.

Whenever a new party came into power, the old postmaster would clean out his desk, remove the pictures off the wall, and move them down to the office of assistant postmaster. The former assistant postmaster would then take his belongings to the office of postmaster, place a picture of the new president on the wall, dust off his old nameplates, and assume his position as the new postmaster.

In a small town, these positions were fairly prestigious. One of these gentlemen was also the chairman of the March of Dimes Charity for the area, a position he had held for quite a few years. I have forgotten the political party that he was affiliated with, although it makes no difference. Honesty and dishonesty are personal attributes, and certainly, no political party has cornered the market on either.

One day, we heard a rumor that there was money missing from the March of Dimes funds and that an investigation and audit were about to be launched. In a small town, this type of rumor spreads very fast, somewhat like wildfire. Not unlike the fire that started in the chairman's garage not too long after this revelation. It appeared somewhat suspicious, and it was later discovered that this was where all the financial records for the charity were stored, and they went up in smoke.

Well, that could have been the end of the story, but apparently, all the records were not destroyed, and along with other data that was available, there was enough information provided to establish that, in fact, some of the funds had been misappropriated, and the chairman would be charged with theft.

Let me digress for a moment. The chairman up to that time had been a pillar of the community, a good church-going family man, my own relationship with him as boss/ employee had been pleasant and enjoyable.

The uproar caused in the small community by the outraged citizens was just as if the chairman had stolen the crutches from under the kids that the March of Dimes was set up to help. It appears that sometimes when a supposedly decent man falls, we can be more vindictive and outraged than the situation might normally justify.

The end of this story is as follows. The chairman's family made restitution for the money that was determined to be short, and he pleaded guilty to the offense.

This was the man's first offense, and as noted previously, he had always been a pillar of the community. If it had been up to the local outraged citizens, he would have at best been sent to prison for life and, at worst, met an immediate untimely end. Fortunately, the judge, in his wisdom, used what appeared to be an old English feudal law to base the punishment on, and the chairman was banished for a term of some years from the city.

This lapse of judgment and access to cash with few controls caused an otherwise good man to stumble and pay a penalty much greater than the amount that was taken.

I believe in these situations that we sometimes relish in the discomfort of others. Especially those to whom we once looked up to only to discover they, too, are only human. We can look at ourselves knowing that we could never do such a thing. Well, I applaud you for the faith you have in yourself, and I hope you never have to be tested.

It is at times like this when you find out who your friends are, or conversely where in the hell did they go.

CHAPTER FIVE

Little Things Made Easy Lead to Larger Things that Can Be Your Downfall

I worked for many years for a large construction company that performed heavy and highway construction work in the western states. I held many positions within the company; however at the time of this incident, I had a fairly insignificant position. Bob (not a real name), the subject of this story, worked in the accounts payable department of the company and was a likable and outgoing fellow, pleasant to work with, and fun to be around, although he appeared not to be the sharpest knife in the drawer.

The heading notes that sometimes little things made easy can lead to larger problems. The little thing in this case was a small accordion file of unclaimed checks that resided on a file cabinet in the accounting department. Construction workers, in many cases, are a fairly transient group, and for whatever reason, if an employee was not present on payday to claim their check, the check was returned to the office and placed into this file to be claimed if and when they should show up again. In many cases, these checks went unclaimed.

There were certainly payroll controls in effect such as randomly accompanying the foreman in handing out checks to make sure that there was an employee for every check and that there were no phantom employees on the payroll. On those occasions, the checks that were unclaimed and unaccounted for were held in a different area to be either claimed by the employee when he showed up, or held until the reason they were not was determined. However, in most cases, the unclaimed checks were relegated to the little accordion file.

This file of unclaimed checks became a source of additional income for Bob as well as the beginning of his downfall. He was careful to the extent that he made sure that the checks that he took were fairly old so that there was a pretty good chance they would probably never be claimed.

The old oxymoron of a victimless crime might even apply here. The case could be made that it was not stealing from the company as the checks had been issued for work that had been completed. The employee that performed the work for whatever reason decided not to pick up the check. There could be a variety of reasons for not doing so. The employee may have over imbibed causing a couple of days' work to be missed and became too embarrassed to show up to pick up the check, or he may have won the lottery, or had come into a substantial inheritance. In any case, the check was apparently not needed.

Now Bob was doing pretty good with the unclaimed check scheme, and it was almost too easy. But it seemed that even this, along with his own regular payroll check, was not enough to keep him in spending money as, for whatever reason, his expenses were increasing, and he needed more. It was then that he decided that with a little more effort, he might even do better. This time, he devised a scheme that produced much greater rewards, but in this case, it was larceny, pure and simple.

The new scheme was not rocket science by any means. Bob simply set up a nonexistent vendor that he controlled and invoiced the company for its services. He would then charge it to one of the ongoing projects as he controlled the approval for payments to vendors.

Once in a while, a project manager or superintendent would peruse the costs for his job, and if it was a large amount to a vendor that he was unfamiliar with, he would come to Bob and question the charge. Bob would then tell him that he would check it out and get back to him. Bob would later report back that the charge had been improperly coded and should have been charged to a different project, and he would take care of it. This satisfied the questioner, and it would be charged to a different project, usually one in which a manager might be somewhat lax in auditing.

The conclusion of this story goes like this. Bob had squirreled away enough money to set himself up in a business and left the company. The problem was that after he was gone, he was not able to cover his tracks when one of his old charges surfaced on a project, and the project manager went to the office manager to resolve the problem. Their discussion also noted how the project manager was totally unfamiliar with the vendor and an expense this large would be very unusual to an unknown vendor. The resulting audit exposed the fraud.

Again, had Bob been satisfied with the smaller larceny of the unclaimed payroll checks, he may have never been caught. But as he became more greedy and more confident and the amounts got bigger and bigger, it was only a matter of time before his scheme was uncovered.

This was somewhat embarrassing to the controller, the office manager, the auditors, and all those responsible for the safeguarding of the company cookie jar, and if a firing squad had been needed, they would have gladly volunteered and even to the extent of furnishing their own guns and bullets. Bob was found guilty and spent some time in prison.

There are now more stringent controls in place including the division of duties, additional approvals for payments, and so on. Had these controls been in place during Bob's tenure, this may never have happened. But in that case, I would not have had this story.

The larger the take as well as the frequency of the take increases the chance that you will serve time if caught. Small amounts can be forgiven. Larger amounts increase the significance of the crime and can also cause those in charge of keeping the lid tight on the company cookie jar to have their own competence questioned, and in some instances, their heads might also roll.

Another consequence of having company funds compromised is that it appears to cause a new attitude of distrust to take place within the company. For a time, at least, it seems that every policy and procedure is reviewed, and in some cases, new ones are added, or old ones tightened up. This problem will not happen again. Everyone is under the microscope.

Hopefully, this is usually a short-term inconvenience, and it, too, will pass. A company theft, especially by its own employee, is not pleasant thing, and it takes time to get over it and, more importantly, to make sure that it does not happen again.

CHAPTER SIX

Do We Make People Thieves if It Is
Expedient and the Savings Fall to the Bottom
Line? After All, It Is Only a Shovel

I don't know if we as a people are inherently crooked, or if we just enjoy the thrill of getting away with something. I think in many cases, it is the latter. I, once again, will be using a construction company background for this story. The item in question is a shovel. I use this as it is somewhat more valuable than a pencil or a pen or stapler or other office supplies, and it falls into a value range of probably twenty-five dollars or more and an amount that I would hope most people would think twice about taking.

The problem arose when shovels kept disappearing on a project. There were thirty employees on the project, and all required a shovel. So far, there had been thirty-five shovels issued, and each day, it would seem that one or more of the employees would report a stolen or misplaced shovel, and another would have to be issued.

The problem at hand is how to control shovels. Do we have each employee sign out for a shovel at the start of the shift and then return it at the end of the shift? This would cause an extra employee and maybe an additional storage facility. Being union employees, they would need to check in and check out the shovels while they were on the clock, and this would continue to happen each day for the duration of the job and would result in a considerable loss of productivity as well as the additional expense that would be incurred. Or do we continue issuing shovels as needed until each employee has a shovel for work and maybe one or two for his home?

The powers to be weighed over the two options and decided that the solution would be to use the second method and hopefully in time the run-on shovels would abate. After a little over double the amount of shovels needed had been issued, it appeared that the run on shovels had stopped, and in the long-run considerable, more money was saved than trying to account for each and every shovel and keep everyone honest.

Did we make thieves out of our employees or contribute to their delinquency in some way? I suppose that we did. Each shovel that left the jobsite and found a new home in an employee's toolshed was a theft. Did we have an obligation to keep the employees honest even if in so doing causes the company to lose money? I think in the pure business sense that preventing the company from losing money trumps most issues.

I do not know the ethical answer to this problem. I do know that somewhere between taking a shovel and a pickup truck, there is a line that must not be crossed. If the speed limit is fifty miles per hour, I would hope that traveling fifty-five would not result in a ticket but would not be surprised if at sixty, a ticket was issued. Either way, we are breaking the letter of the law. The spirit of the law, however, does have some leeway. I would also hope that if there is a Judgment Day, a bit of wiggle room might be allowed on our behalf.

CHAPTER SEVEN

Let's Scare the Hell Out of the Employees and
See if We Can Slow Down the Pilferage

This is a similar problem to that addressed in the previous chapter. Management assumed, and rightfully so, that office supplies and various other items were being appropriated by the employees for their personal use.

We as employees, after all, are only human, and whatever supplies we might have taken can easily be rationalized as something owed to us for the extra time and effort that we have put in thinking about work on the way home, at home, or over dinner. This is just deferred compensation due us and is certainly only a small partial payment for all the unpaid time and effort that we have expended for the benefit of our jobs.

Most companies I have worked for have an employee that it uses to test the water for any new system, policy, or work rule that it plans to implement. This employee is told confidentially of the new idea. He has no idea that he is being used as a management tool. He then passes the information on to other employees individually and confidentially as though each of them is the only one privy to the information. It is amazing the feedback that management will receive.

Management or a management consultant came up with the following idea. The employee described above is called into a management meeting and is asked his opinion of the following plan. He is told that the company had decided to submit all employees to a lie detector test. They would be asked questions as to what they had removed (swiped) from the office during the past year for their personal use, and he was asked to give his thoughts on and asked what he thought of this idea.

The enlisted employee, before discussing it with any of the other employees, decided to give himself a test. It was surprising the amount that he came up with. The first things that you think about are basic office supplies such as pens, pencils, staplers, binders, and so on. However, when questioned about travel, expense accounts, petty cash reimbursements, overtime, etc., the fictitious items can add up to a surprisingly large amount.

Now, the enlisted employee, armed with the plans of management to have all employees subjected to a lie detector as well as the somewhat significant total of the items that he himself had taken, proceeded to share this with the other employees. He met individually and in his usually secretive way and explained the plan to the other employees.

I do not believe it was ever envisioned or intended that the plan was to be actually carried out. I think that it was management's way of showing concern for the expenditures and hoping to scare the employees into being a little less larcenous for fear this little exercise would actually happen. As I have said before, adults are just older and larger children, and this appears to be a somewhat sophomoric attempt to solve the problem.

The results of this little exercise are unknown or, in any case, were too difficult to measure. This little exercise serves only to point out that this is an ongoing problem whether in the office of a small church, or a megacorporation.

Pilferage is just another, maybe kinder, name for stealing, shoplifting, etc. and is committed by both employees and customers. It is nearly impossible to prevent this type of theft without major expenditures only to catch the few determined culprits. Even though many of us appear to have a somewhat larcenous nature, the possibility and embarrassment of being caught keeps most of us honest.

Therefore, other than those eyes and ears that were already in place at the store, factory, office, etc., it was determined that it was much easier and less costly to add an additional markup to whatever the product or service that the company produced to cover the cost of this pilferage.

This is another instance in which the cost to prevent theft is much greater than the actual costs of the items that will be stolen. Therefore, it is tolerated.

CHAPTER EIGHT

A Theft that Keeps on Giving and Giving, or
Grab Something that Is Needed, Repackage It,
and Rent It, or Sell It Back to Your Employer

I remember this incident from a summer job that I had while going to school. I actually believe that it may have begun somewhat innocently.

As I recall, an employee was going to do a personal weekend job for some extra money, and he needed concrete forms for the job; however, he did not want to rent them as that would cut into his profit. So on Friday evening, he loaded some of the company forms onto his truck and took them home with him to do the job. This was probably done with the thought of returning them when the job was completed. Somehow, however, this must have slipped his mind, and they were not returned.

Sometime later, the company came up short in the amount of forms that were needed to complete a job. The above employee notified the foreman that he had enough of the type of forms needed at home to complete the job, and he would be happy to rent them to the company for the duration of the job.

I don't know if the humor of this is appreciated or not, and I am sure it would not be by the company owner. The forms had been stenciled with the initials of the company prior to their being purloined. And the borrower of the forms prior to renting them back to the company had tried to cover up these identifying marks, and he roughly spray-painted over the old company initials. He was probably trying to save on paint and did not do a very good job and some of the original identification remained, although barely legible.

Well, we end this little incident with the foreman confronting the culprit and letting him know that it appeared that he was renting the company's own forms. The culprit denied this and claimed that he had purchased the forms some time ago but could not remember from whom. The foreman then proceeded to point out the barely legible company initials that were still visible on some of the forms.

The employee was now somewhat shaken. It was now not only the question of the stolen forms, but the employee's job was on the line. He again assured the foreman that he came by the forms innocently, although he agreed that they were probably stolen. He admitted that the situation appeared awkward but hoped the return of the forms to the company would show his heart was in the right place.

The employee was not discharged. He had been a valuable and productive employee for the company up to that time, and the foreman, to his credit, decided against his dismissal and no more was said, and a lesson was hopefully learned.

As far as the end of the story, I can only say that I know that at least three years later, the employee was still working for the company. I know in some instances an employee caught in a situation like this can harbor a grudge for a long time and would probably be better off to have been let go. In other instances, and most I hope, the employee appreciates the second chance given him and becomes an even more valuable and loyal employee. As in most things in life, these situations are a judgment call.

Good luck, hire the best employees that you can, and hope for the best. If you are lucky, it may not happen to you but don't bet on it.

CHAPTER NINE

The Real Estate Industry Prior to the Crash
Fueled Many Financial Opportunities for Banks,
Mortgage Companies, Individuals, and Others

The events leading up to the real estate crash, crisis, bubble, pop, debacle, or whatever you want to call it, was fueled with many opportunities to get rich. Even greater opportunities arose for those who were somewhat willing to stretch the truth, and it seemed everybody did. After all, when everyone is doing it, and we are just part of the crowd, our conscience is somewhat eased. A wink here and a wink there, and life was good. The rewards become even greater, and those questionable activities became part of the norm. It was a time when everyone was making money: the real estate agents and brokers, appraisers, home inspectors, the banks, the mortgage companies, contractors, Wall Street, rating agencies, and individuals.

The banks and mortgage companies held their loan officers feet to the fire to produce more loans, or be replaced. Stated income was accepted from mortgage applicants. That meant that they could claim any amount of income on the loan application, and it need not be verified. The box on the form should have been titled overstated income.

Contracts were made with applicants to build new homes with the understanding that they would occupy them upon completion. The reality of it was that they had no intention of living in them, and the home would be put on the market and sold upon completion. This appeared to most as only a small technicality and again was winked at by those involved in the practice.

This was a method that was used by both individuals to build homes one at a time as well as by contractors that would line up folks with good credit ratings to allow him to make contracts for a larger number of homes for which the straw buyers would receive a specified amount or a percent of the sales price when they were completed and sold.

People were buying homes and adding a coat of paint or other cosmetic improvement or, in some cases, doing nothing and merely reselling them at a profit within a very short time (flipping).

The loans were bundled together (securitized) for a fee by Wall Street firms and sold to investors, thereby allowing the banks to free up their capital so that they could start lending money all over again. Rating agencies were giving these products their rubber stamped seal of approval, and in hindsight, the vast amount of fees that they collected appeared to have somewhat clouded their judgment. But then again, money will do that.

This was a time when you were crazy not to be in real estate. Real estate prices were increasing by double digits every year. There was always a market for residential homes. And if you were not participating, you were just plain dumb. Housewives, who gathered together for morning coffee, got involved and pooled their monies and bought older run-down homes or bought lots and hired contractors to remodel or build a new home.

It was not even necessary to be involved in any of these shenanigans to be rewarded. Your home became a bank account that just continued to grow. If it was worth $150,000 a few years ago, it had jumped to $175,000 the following year and $200,000 or more the next year. This was like money in the bank just waiting to be tapped. Now you traded in your old Chevy or Ford for a new Buick or Lexus to match the value of your home. Instead of going to Disneyland, Europe, and other exotic locations became the vacation spots of choice.

The money was withdrawn by refinancing your home, and this became an annual rite of passage. In the event that you did not want to refinance the total amount and have to pay the additional costs involved, a home equity was taken out at little or no additional cost. The lower interest rates had little noticeable effect to the monthly mortgage payment. And in some cases, with the lower interest rates, the payment would even decrease.

Everyone was getting rich, fat, and happy during this frenzy. Life was good. What could possibly go wrong?

Well, when the last buyer standing had purchased his home, we soon found out. The real estate market collapsed. New homes and remodeled homes came onto the market with no buyers, and many remained empty and unsold for a long time. Large and small subdivisions with streets, sidewalks, and utilities sat idle with very few, if any, homes. The stated income homeowners that had overstated their income were unable to make their house payments.

This also applied to those who withdrew their growing equity annually through refinancing or home equity loans to pay for cars, boats, vacations, and other items to be amortized along with the home over a thirty-year period. The value of the loans exceeded the value of their home (underwater).

The straw buyers who had homes built with the intention of a quick sale now had two or more mortgages that could not be paid. The Wall Street created securities backed by mortgages were worth much less than originally thought when they were created. The Triple A ratings that these securities received from the rating agencies that gave them sense of legitimacy did not mean much at this time.

The employees of banks, mortgage companies, title companies, real estate salesman, appraisers, home inspectors, and contractors were given prison time at worst or were bankrupted, put out of work, or severely downsized at best.

I do not know of anyone that has not been affected by this catastrophe either directly or indirectly. Whether it be from a loss of a job to the diminished value of their homes as well as that of their investments and retirement accounts and other assets. Our state, local, and national economies also suffered from lack of tax revenue due to a shrinkage of the revenue base both of property taxes and out-of-work individuals. Additional money was printed to bail out the too-large-to-fail banks, automobile, and insurance companies.

There was a lesson to be learned through all this as we look back upon the events as they unfolded. The advantage of twenty-twenty hindsight does a wonderful job of pointing this out.

How did we not see the warning flags? We knew that double-digit inflation of home prices could not continue forever, interest rates were at the lowest they had been in many years, a supply of homes on the market that most people could not afford, and the supply far outstripping the demand. Sooner or later, everything had to come to a screeching halt.

This was one case or example in which most everyone involved in real estate broke the rules. It began with the top officials in the industry condoning, encouraging, and even threatening those who did not participate in the subterfuge known as the real estate industry. It continued right on down to the bottom rung of the real estate ladder to the lowest entry-level loan officers, bank employees, appraisers, etc.

It was next to impossible to participate and compete as an honest broker, banker, contractor, or investor. Everyone appeared to turn a blind eye to the conditions that abounded throughout every phase of the real estate industry. Whatever it was called, greed, avarice, or just the ability to compete, survive, and exist in the industry, in most cases, your better judgment was compromised, and you joined the crowd. It was just like a gold mine with a finite amount of ore. When it was gone, there was no more, and everyone was after theirs before the supply ran out.

The crowd mentality appears to be if everyone is participating, it is not wrong. There is safety in numbers and comfort in being part of the group. They can't put all of us in jail. That is true and they did not. There were very few-and-far-between cases of serious punishment. It seems to prove that there is safety in numbers and being part of the group. It did, however, bring the country to the verge of a serious depression.

We can all take comfort in the old saying "misery loves company," and there was certainly enough misery and company to go around. But we live in a great, resilient, albeit impatient country, and we will get our act together and get out of this mess.

Will it happen again? Of course, it will. We relive history over and over again, just check with the Dutch on the price of tulips. After all, we are only human.

CHAPTER TEN

Unions: Comments, Platitudes, and Complaints

Let me begin by going on record and saying that part of the greatness of this country can be attributed to the labor union movement. The company owners and business magnates that were instrumental in creating this great country were no friend to the workingman. Those monies paid to the workers were that much less that went into their pockets. To this day, all laboring people, in a big part, can thank the labor union movement for their wages, working conditions, working hours, and the benefits that they receive.

The pendulum occasionally swings too far toward one group or the other, but due to vigilance from both sides with both complaining they are getting the short end of the stick, it appears to be working. Labor laws and working conditions that all of us, both union and nonunion, take for granted were fought for and won by our labor union movement.

I am not and have never been a member of a union. I have worked in industries that the labor force was fully unionized, and it appeared that the nonunion side of the company also benefited from the higher wages and benefits of the union workers.

I do not want to get into any philosophical debates over the pluses and minuses of the union. I will only state my experiences and let you, dear reader, draw your own conclusions.

My first experience with a union was, as mentioned in chapter four, regarding my employment at the post office. I will not restate it here only to say that I believe that it was more of a union in name only as certain union tools were not allowed, and these included strikes, work slowdowns, and so on. I will, however, comment on government entities being union a little later.

My next experience occurred while working on a construction project. Most of the workforce on the project had previously worked for a large mining concern and been temporarily laid off. The thing I most noticed was the intense dislike that many of the employees shared and voiced for their former employer. I couldn't help but wonder, with feelings like that, *Why would they even work for such a company?* However, when the old employer started hiring again, and an employee's name came up for reinstatement, they immediately resigned and went back to their old job. The benefits and wages that were received upon returning could not be overlooked. Again, the happy worker is a complaining worker. Go figure.

The following problem was reported to me by an employee who worked in security for the mining company noted in the preceding paragraph. He commented on how it was almost impossible to charge a union employee with theft even when he was caught red-handed unless there were at least two or more witnesses, and even then, the union would back the employee every time. I know that there always appears to be a constant state of antagonism between labor and management. But a thief would appear to be a thief in either camp; however, this was obviously not the case.

Finally, and of course, another story from the construction industry. This time, a construction crew was working on a highway project. The project was to replace a storm drain that ran under the street. Each residence along the way would lose access to their driveway as the pipe was being laid past their property.

It was during this time that the business agent from the union drove up and told the crew that a strike had been called, and they were to walk off the job immediately. The strike was to be industry wide and had nothing to do with this particular project.

The job was less than hour from being complete whereby the property owner would have access to his driveway. The job superintendent intervened and suggested that they should probably at least finish the job to the point that enabled a property owner to have access to his driveway, or possibly they may never work for the company again.

I have stated the intent of his words; however, it is possible that the superintendent's actual words were somewhat more descriptive and colorful than stated. Well, in any case, there was a meeting of the minds, and the workers completed the access to the driveway prior to walking off the job.

This appeared to be reasonable request, and all parties were to be commended. The threat by the superintendent was probably not enforceable, but it appears that occasionally, common sense can prevail.

Regardless of the craziness and outrageous demands that we often hear during the collective bargaining process, I continue to believe that unions are necessary and will continue to have their place representing the workingman as well as leveling the playing field in many industries. As I stated earlier, whether an employee is union or not, the benefits, conditions, work rules, and wages received by everyone are largely due to the union movement.

I am not going to get into a philosophical debate over union membership. I must, however, throw out some thoughts on the good folks that work for our benevolent government entities, be it federal, state, county, city, town, or whatever.

I am not a big believer, or believer at all, in government employees belonging to a union. The benefits provided, the wages paid, and the almost-guaranteed job security that government employees are already provided are those same things that the unions fought for in the first place.

Furthermore, the thought of being held hostage by a government union, whether by sanitation workers turning a city into a huge garbage dump or airports or other government transportation being closed down by striking union members, is not an option that should in any way be tolerated.

Somewhere along the line, I probably have missed something in the argument for government unions. However, I do not understand the need for union representation for government employees as I have noted above. These are just my current feelings. I have not done a lot of study, nor have I lost much sleep over it. And I have yet to hear of one reasonable argument in favor of the unionization of government employees that has in any way persuaded me to change my views.

Somehow the government appears to be getting further and further away from us common folk, and government unionization appears to be just another step in that direction.

CHAPTER ELEVEN

Just How Much Is a Job Worth?

This event seems very similar to the old railroad engine repair joke, and for those of you who may be unfamiliar with it or have been off the planet for some time, it goes like this.

As I best I can remember, a mechanic was called to repair a stalled train engine. Upon arriving at the site, he looked at the engine from all angles, walked around it a couple of times, and then got out a hammer. He went up to the engine, carefully selected a spot, and then hit it once with his hammer. The engine was immediately able to be started.

The total elapsed time for this was probably less than ten minutes. The mechanic submitted a bill for $300. The bill seemed quite high for the time expended, and the bill was sent back requesting the charges to be itemized. The mechanic then sent back the following: labor $5, knowing where to tap the engine $295. This is a very old joke, and I hope by now, it is public domain.

A similar type of situation arose at a bank. It seems that a local small-town bank had purchased a new safe, and it had just been installed. The problem arose the following morning when they went to open the safe to get the money for the day's business. The combination or whatever method that was used to open the safe had been taken by the installers.

A phone call to the manufacturer of the safe was made, and they were informed that the installers would have to return to correct the situation, and the soonest that they could return was the following day.

After a high-level meeting with the bank president and other powers that be, a possible solution was placed on the table. There was a person in the community that when his name was mentioned, all agreed that he might just save the day. I cannot go into the reasons why this fellow seemed a unanimous choice, but he was called in.

He arrived at the bank and gave the safe a cursory examination for a few minutes and then told those assembled that he just might be able to solve their dilemma. He went to work with some tools and other paraphernalia that he had brought with him, and to the joy and amazement of the very interested bystanders, he had it opened within a very short time.

The locksmith obviously knew his business and enjoyed the accolades he received from the bank president and the other employees that had assembled.

Well, as the group stood around congratulating themselves and the locksmith on opening the safe, they asked him what the charge would be. I do not remember the amount, but let's say for the sake of discussion, it was $500.

Upon hearing this, the bank president blurted out, "Absolutely not! You were only here for ten minutes."

The locksmith then calmly closed the safe door and said, "Goodbye."

This caused another immediate high-level meeting to be called at which time the amount was reconsidered and even somewhat increased before the locksmith was called back and went to work on the safe again. The safe was once again opened. The locksmith, again, was on the receiving end of the appreciative group of bank management and employees' smiles, thanks, and gratitude and was given a check for his services.

When you are having a medical problem, and there is only one doctor in town, you don't have a lot of bargaining power. This can also be said when in need of the services of a lone mechanic, locksmith, or a hamburger at the only café in town. Take it or leave it—that is your only choice.

Hopefully, the day will come when you are the one holding the winning cards. However, until that day comes, it pays to hold your tongue as you are the only one with anything to lose.

CHAPTER TWELVE

One of the Finest Men that It Has Been
My Fortune to Have Known

I respected the judge from the first moment that I became
acquainted with him as a young lad, and this respect has
become greater as I have grown older and discovered more
of his deeds and accomplishments. I grew up as his neighbor, and his son was and still is my good friend. As young
boys, we do not fully comprehend the greatness of indi-

viduals only as in how they relate to you. He was a district judge who presided over three counties in our state.

As a boy, I would join him and his son on trips into some of the more remote and desolate parts of the county. He loved the desert and the mountains, and I learned much of the history of the area while on these excursions.

I remember one occasion when he took us to a remote area where he stopped and showed us a mining claim he had staked out. There was an old tin Prince–Albert–Tobacco can under a pile of rocks with a map inside that gave the boundaries of the claim.

We also received history lessons of the early settlers, the Indians, the miners, and other stories, highlights, and information regarding the history and landmarks of the area.

It was not until later that I learned the judge's father and uncle were also early lawyers and judges in the area. That his law school education was self-taught, and upon completion, he passed the bar. He had been both an active and reserve officer in the Army Judge Advocate General's Corps and retired as a full colonel. During World War II, he was appointed the military governor of one of the Hawaiian Islands and saw duty throughout the South Pacific.

One thing that set him apart from other judges in the state was his refusal to wear the judicial robes that most of the other judges wore. He would wear a business suit as he presided over his court. Other judges and officials tried to get him to comply with official dress code, but he refused. I believe that his reasoning was that because most of the courts, over which he presided, were located in smaller towns, and the citizenry might think the robe was somewhat over the top. His office was an elective one, and I do not believe that he ever lost an election.

Here are a few cases and incidents that give me faith in our justice system, at least in his court. Although, they may or may not all relate to the tone of this book, but I believe that it shows at least his fair-mindedness and respect of the law.

I mentioned him in a previous chapter with regard to the March of Dimes official that misappropriated some of the funds. His was the court that presided over the trial.

One of his cases involved a black lady on trial for demonstrating in a small college town in his jurisdiction. The total population of blacks in the town could be counted on both hands with a couple of fingers left over and would have included those black players on the football and basketball teams for the college. As the trial progressed, it was clear that the defendant was being railroaded. The discrimination exhibited was blatant. It was a jury trial, and sure enough, after a very short deliberation, the verdict was delivered, and it was guilty.

After the judge explained the verdict to the defendant, he then explained to the defendant the steps necessary to appeal the case and told her that if she ran into any problems, she could contact his office at any time. They would provide her whatever assistance she needed to prepare the appeal.

The case was appealed and was dismissed.

There was another case in which two neighbors were having a conflict. This was also in a small town and almost everyone knew one another. A dispute between two neighbors had escalated to the point that finally one of them filed a lawsuit.

It was just before the trial was to begin when the gentleman that had filed the lawsuit arrived in the courtroom. The judge approached him and called him by name. He told him to go into his chambers and that there was an open lawbook on his desk. He was told to read the paragraph that was above the ruler that the judge had placed in the open book.

The man went into the chambers, and after a few minutes, he returned to the courtroom. He told the judge that after reading the paragraph that it appeared he had a pretty weak case, and he withdrew the lawsuit. The end of the story is that the two parties to the lawsuit settled their problem in the hallway outside the courtroom.

The judge did not advise or council the man in any way other than letting him make up his own mind regarding the point of law that was in contention. Time and money were not wasted on a trial, and maybe some feelings saved that might have been injured during a trial.

My last example will be that of yet another government entity being compromised, in this case, a school district. Again, when we are dealing with hard cash with little or no controls, our threshold for larceny drops dramatically. There are not many cases within school districts in which actual cash money is just found lying around. That is unless you think of those selling tickets for say a high school football, basketball, or other athletic event.

There was a school employee that was placed in charge of selling the tickets, counting money, and making up the deposit for the revenue from the games. She was a single woman and that probably was the criteria for selecting her for the assignment. Other school employees were married and had families and did not want to put in the extra time that was needed. The first time she did this job was as an assignment. Thereafter, she simply volunteered for this duty until it was assumed that this was her job, and she continued in this capacity for many years. I wonder why. That is until, I suppose, someone started checking ticket numbers and multiplying them by the ticket cost and finding a large discrepancy in what was deposited and what should have been.

This little scheme had continued for such a long period of time, the actual amount of money taken was unable to be determined. The guilty person was charged with a much smaller amount than was actually taken. This is not uncommon and is usually what happens in these types of cases.

The trial found her guilty of misappropriating school funds. The judge felt that due to the many years over which this crime had taken place that prison time was appropriate. She was sentenced to a prison term.

Again, had she been caught on the first attempt, there would probably have been no prison time, and restitution could have been made and could possibly have even retained her job. More importantly, had the school officials in charge set up more stringent controls, there would have been no crime. And again, no story.

CHAPTER THIRTEEN

What in the Hell Was I Thinking?
and My Day in Court

My current occupation is that of a real estate appraiser, and business for a time ranged from slow to almost nonexistent. This can be attributed to the problems as noted in a previous chapter, and this is where the following experiences were derived from. The first is included to illustrate that it is not necessary to demand a pound of flesh for every infraction. I was impressed how the problem was handled.

Following this is a rogue government entity in action trying to steam roll over anyone gets in its way.

There are certain guidelines and standards to be followed when preparing a real estate appraisal. An example of this would be that the comparable sales selected should be current sales, similar in size, age, location, and amenities, wherever possible, to the home being appraised. When this is not possible, an explanation must be included as to why not, and there are other procedures and so on that must be followed.

Each state has its own board to govern appraisers and to see that the guidelines and standards are followed and enforced as needed.

As appraisers, we try to be attentive to the requirements for appraisal preparation as being called before the board can be a somewhat traumatic experience. Everyone in this business has probably at least one appraisal in our past that we were in such a hurry with, overlooked something, or left something out, and in any case, we wish could have it back. This would not have been intentional but things happen.

There are horror stories about being subjected to the grilling of the board, treated like a criminal, assumed that you intentionally broke the rules and regulations, so on and so forth, and that when you leave, it may or may not be with your license still intact.

This is why the following story about an appraiser from a neighboring state that had been called before the board caught my attention. The appraiser received his notice of a complaint against him and was notified to appear before the board. He appeared as instructed at the time and place set up for his hearing. He went into the room, and to his surprise, there was only one board member present. As he walked in, the board member arose and approached him and put his arm around him and called him by name and said, "This is the only complaint that has ever been filed against you. You know better than this. Don't let it happen again," and with these words of admonishment, he was excused.

I like and included this story for a couple of reasons, the first being that an appraiser's previous work history had been consulted and had been appreciated. The second is that it did not belittle or shame the person who already assumedly felt pretty bad, and he left feeling that his self-worth was still intact.

This type of settling a problem may not work in every instance. Usually, it can only apply to a first offense of an individual with an otherwise satisfactory work history and other redeeming qualities. These, along with the judgment of a superior, could result in a teaching lesson to a future valuable appraiser. Or it may not; however, if it appears the individual is truly sorry and contrite, let us err on the side of compassion.

The time and money that has been expended to train a person up to the point of the problem should not be overlooked. If it appears that the individual deserves a second chance, go for it. If not, go ahead and cut your losses.

Let me set up the next story. I had a complaint filed against me; however, it was not to be settled before an appraisal board. It was to be settled in a courtroom. The gist of it was this. There was a group of cabins located on a small patch of private land surrounded by government-owned land and residing on a mountainside within a ski resort.

It appears that this small group was a thorn in the side of the local government. There were probably half-dozen-or-so cabins in the development, and most had been there for at least the last fifty years.

Every year, the county would assess a value for taxes on these cabins that was much greater than the market value. And every year, the owners would hire an appraiser to present their side of the case. I represented the homeowners for a few years, and each year succeeded in getting the taxes lowered significantly. This little exercise went on year after year. The final year that I was involved with this, the county filed a complaint against me to the appraisal board and then took the tax issue to a higher court.

I had to appear in court to defend my appraisals. The county appraiser and his supervisor appeared along with myself and a few of the homeowners that I represented.

Let me just explain a bit about the cabins in question. The cabins had electricity, spring-fed water in the summer, and no water or road access in the winter. The homeowners were a bunch of pretty rugged individuals, and the cabins were used mainly in the winter for skiing. There was no winter access to the cabins other than by skis or snowshoes. All supplies, including food and water, were brought up in this manner.

I was on the stand and explained the situation to the judge. The county people acknowledged that this was true. However, they said that I could not argue that these were not ski-in-ski-out properties, and these types of properties are much more valuable than the values that I had appraised. I admitted that in the literal sense of ski-in-ski-out that they certainly were. I then explained to the court that a typical ski-in-ski-out property similar to those in the larger neighboring and nearby resorts allowed you to drive your car to the front door or into a heated garage and unload your gear. You would have running water, heat, appliances, and other amenities similar to being at home. And when it was time you donned, your skis stepped out the door for a day of skiing and upon completion skied back to the property. The cabins that I represented were comparable in name only.

It was at this point that the county appraiser began shouting questions at me. His supervisor then joined in, and I was attempting to answer both of them, and no one was able to be understood. It was at this time that one of the homeowners that had accompanied me then raised his hand and got the judge's attention. He identified himself as also being a judge and commented that in his courtroom, only one person at a time was allowed to talk. The presiding judge then said that he had heard enough and ruled in our favor.

The reason that I have included this little story is to validate the old saying, "You can't fight city hall." I feel sorry for the homeowners as they will have to continue to fight this every year. You really can't fight city hall.

The harassment that I encountered during this particular time made me think twice about representing the homeowners any longer. I decided that it was not worth my time, effort, and worry. The ruling in the case caused the dismissal of the complaint that the county had filed against me at the appraisal board.

Government entities are usually run by career bureaucrats and are really beholding to no one. They follow the laws if it is convenient, and if it is not, you can go to hell. Forgive me if I add one more case just to get it off my chest.

I did some work for a private attorney, and he let me know up front that he would pay one half of the appraisal fee, and the state would pay the other half. Guess which one would not pay? You got it. After several attempts, the state sent me a letter notifying me that until the case was settled, they would not pay their portion of the fee. The law and policy is that upon completion of an appraisal, the fee is due and payable. The fee is not contingent with any outcome or judgment. What are you going to do? Write a book, I guess.

CHAPTER FOURTEEN

God Bless the ATM

There is very little need to go inside a bank anymore since the advent of the automated teller machines. I usually make both deposits and withdrawals from my car window to the nameless faceless ATM at my bank, and it is usually much faster and more convenient than waiting in line for a teller. Isn't technology grand?

I used to assume that there was somewhat more intelligence built into the ATM machine than there actually was. It is very good at counting out twenty-dollar bills, or so it seemed for a long time. It only dispenses one denomination of bill and that is the twenty-dollar bill. I again assumed that every time a bill popped out of the damn machine that it knew that it was a twenty-dollar bill. We sometimes place too much trust in technology, and I have since discovered that this is not true.

I typically withdraw amounts of one hundred dollars, and it has always been delivered as five twenty-dollar bills. That is until the time that I entered a withdrawal amount for one hundred dollars and received four twenty-dollar bills and a five-dollar bill. I thought that maybe the machine had run out of cash and had given me what was left. I checked the receipt, however, and one hundred dollars have been deducted from my account.

Somewhere there is an employee that stacks twenty-dollar bills into neat little bundles to be loaded into these machines. I would suppose that there is another employee on duty in the hopes of keeping each other honest. In any case, by hook or by crook, a five-dollar bill had been slipped into the stack, and the stackers probably had lunch on me that day.

The modern ATM machine, to its credit, counted out five pieces of paper as it was built to do and would have been correct had each been a twenty-dollar bill. Had I just placed the money in my pocket and driven off, I probably would never have been the wiser. However, having worked in the computer world before, I know things are not always as they appear, so I am somewhat alert to these things, or I guess I am a bit anal.

Anyway, this is not a great amount, and it was after hours. But when you are not responsible for the computer error as I had been many times in my career, I thought I might enjoy pointing out the problem to the bank and that they might even appreciate knowing that there could be a problem.

So there I was at the bank bright and early the next morning and explained my dilemma. I was subjected to a grilling by a bank official who questioned my honesty and integrity for some time before finally conceding that this could possibly happen and apparently did. The bank then credited my account with the fifteen-dollar difference.

The ATM Gets Its Due

There is a large parking area around a nearby mall where I live. A neighbor and I would often walk our dogs there in the mornings before work and before the mall opened. We would meet occasionally although he would usually arrive earlier and be gone before I came along.

One morning, there were police cars blocking access to the area in which I usually walk, and I was unable to use the lot that morning. I saw my neighbor a few days later and asked him if he knew what had happened. He explained that he arrived just about the same time as the police. They had been called to the area to investigate a complaint of someone beating on an object in the early morning hours with a sledgehammer. Upon the arrival of the police, the individual or individuals that were involved ran off.

The object of the receiving end of the hammer blows was a bank's ATM machine that had been stolen and taken to this somewhat remote spot to try to crack it open to get to the money inside. Apparently, during the design of the ATM, there was some thought given as to this type of problem happening, and they designed a pretty tough machine. The crooks had not been able to compromise the machine, and the money was still inside.

Well, my friend and his dogs continued on their way. A short time later, one of the dogs began scratching and whining at the side of dumpster that was located behind one of the mall stores. Well, my friend lifted the lid and peered in and was met by a pair of eyes staring back. With that, he dropped the lid to the dumpster and secured it and went off to get one of the police officers to further investigate his findings.

The pair of eyes inside the dumpster belonged to one of the culprits that had stolen the ATM machine. The police thanked my friend for his help. They also told him that the state's banking association had a $10,000 standing reward that was offered to anyone that was involved in helping solve a bank robbery.

Now this had a pretty good ring to it both to my friend and in the banking association's advertising campaign. Although my friend was not aware of this prior to involvement, he did apply for it.

I would check with him occasionally to see how the reward was coming, or if he had collected it yet. Well, I guess there were some additional hoops to be jumped through and some other requirements that were hidden away in the small print of the reward requirements that had not been met. In any case, he never received the reward.

There was, however, a somewhat happy ending to the story. My friend was finally awarded a free checking account for life for his assistance. I guess that my advice would be that if you are ever placed in a position of helping solve a bank robbery, rather than place yourself in any danger, think twice, as many banks offer free checking accounts without the hassle.

CHAPTER FIFTEEN

Just When You Think You Have
Seen about Everything

The following is an eclectic collection of snippets that I find interesting and would hope you might also. Some may have no relation to the basic premise of this book, some might, some I just find humorous and, in my opinion, are worth repeating. You obviously will make up your own mind.

Does This Guy Really Need a Company Car?

I went out to a construction job site on a state high-way project to meet with a state official. I went over to the state's job office and parked in front of the trailer, and up on blocks was a car with the motor running in gear with either a speed control set or a weight on the gas pedal. Not being much of a mechanic, I assumed that there was some sort of test being performed on the car.

I was wrong. The state employee, to whom the car was assigned, was due to have his company car replaced. There were two criteria that had to be met in order to receive a new car. The first was that he had to have had the car for a certain period of time, and second, it was to have exceeded a certain amount of mileage. If both of these criteria had been met, he would have been eligible for a new car.

Obviously, one of the criteria had not been met.

What Do You Say to the Boss as He Passes You Seated in First Class as He Heads through to Coach?

You can say whatever you want and then wait for the memo regarding the air travel policy of your company when you get back to the office.

Hopefully, there is no policy in which case there will be one implemented and will probably be named after you. In the case that there is a standing policy, be ready to fork over the difference if you are given the chance between that and the highway. Or on the other hand, if you were on personal business, and the ticket was purchased with your nickel, you are in the clear. However, I would doubt very much that this would be the case in the latter scenario.

Time to Gas Up the Company Car and May as well Take Care of the Family Buggy Too

This is certainly nothing new, but company credit cards have become a license to steal and, in many cases, with very little thought to covering up the trail. If we fill up the company car in the morning, it is probably not too wise to use the same card to fill up the family buggy later in the same day.

If you really want to test the system, fill up the rental car while on vacation in Florida when the company car resides in Oregon. Obviously, these are just a few of many situations that could arise, but we will leave them at this for now.

If, and it probably very seldom happens, you are confronted by the company auditor in one of these situations, the correct answer, of course, would be that you grabbed the wrong credit card by mistake and that you are certainly very sorry and will certainly make up the amount in question. This should cover you in most cases unless it is pointed out to you that this has happened twenty-seven other times during the past year.

And in the case that costs and mileage are kept for each company car and your vehicle has triple the costs of others with similar mileage, a visit from a supervisor could also be expected. Good luck.

This kind of problem appears to be somewhat prevalent within the ranks of those whose jobs are to enforce the law: our policemen, sheriff's departments, highway troopers, and so forth. It seems that in some cases, there is confusion as to whether their position is to enforce the law, or whether they are above the law. Should the personnel holding these jobs be held to a higher level of accountability than others? I think not, more on that later.

Is It Raining Hard Enough to Shut Down the Job and Go Home?

I do not mean to pick on state employees, but it is sometimes so easy. It seems that there needed to be a standard devised so as to determine at what point rain becomes sufficient to shut down a job.

I assume that this problem was tossed around for some time, probably at least for five minutes and maybe somewhat longer and hopefully not a great deal of overtime was expended. The various solutions were submitted, graded for reasonableness and ease of implementation, and other pertinent aspects.

The solution that was decided upon, after great deliberation, was to set a brick out in the open, and if a certain amount of drops showed up on it within a one-minute period, the job was to be shut down, and everyone would go home.

I am sorry that I do not remember the number of drops required or the size of the brick. What would you expect? These guys were engineers.

You Never Know Who You Might Run into even in a Strange Airport in Need of a Restroom

This is an event that I find it extremely coincidental and maybe even a bit humorous. I include this to show that you never know who you might run into, whether it is at the corner grocery store or halfway around the world. So behave yourself wherever you are.

There were two of my male coworkers each on an unrelated business trip, and their paths crossed unknowingly at an airport hundreds of miles from the home office. There was a commotion coming from a ladies' restroom that was near to where one of them was sitting waiting to catch a connecting flight. He looked up to see what was happening just about the time the other was being ushered out of the ladies' restroom and in a none-too-kindly fashion. I should make it perfectly clear that the one exiting the restroom went into the wrong restroom by mistake. These are his words. In any case, what are the odds? It is a small world.

Finally Found that Significant Other: Time to Go Shopping for that Ring

There comes a time when, and for most of us, it is the first time that we visit the jewelry store. We are in the market for a diamond for our future bride, so there we are. In my case, this was one of two small jewelry stores in town.

The shop owner directed me to a small glass top table above a selection of diamond rings. He proceeded to give a short lesson on the four Cs of diamond selection. These were, as I recall, cut, clarity, carat, and color. The first three he covered very quickly. Cut was style such as emerald cut, round cut, etc. Clarity, I think, was the clearness of the stone, blemishes, etc. The carat was the weight (size) of the stone, and he passed over these very quickly.

He then came to the color and explained that the better stones had a slightly bluish tint or color to them. He set some rings on the table of various designs and styles, and all had a bluish color to them as he explained they were the better stones.

He was then called away to a phone call while I continued to inspect the rings. The diamonds all had a bluish color or tint to them that he assured me was the sign of a better diamond. This was some years ago, and there was a clear glass ashtray on the table. I noticed that the ashtray also had a bluish tint to it. I glanced at my watch and noticed that the glass face also had a blue tint to it that I had never noticed before. It was then I looked at the lamp that was on the table and the light bulb beneath the shade was emitting a somewhat blue light.

About this time, the store owner came back to see how I was doing and asked if I had made up mind on a ring yet. I asked him if he was going to throw in the lamp with the purchase of the ring. He looked at me somewhat confused, and I told him I was going to shop around a little more before I made up my mind and left the store.

That Solution Is Too Damn Easy. Why
Couldn't We Think of That?

The Condo Gestapo, also known as the Homeowners
Association in charge of a condominium complex to
which my friend belongs, was having its annual meeting.
Sometimes it seems that there are just not enough problems
to solve, so we sometimes just have to dig a little deeper to
find one, or maybe even make up a few. Otherwise, why in
the world would we have these meetings?

The problem on the table looking for a solution was
what to do about members that do not retrieve their garbage cans from the curb in a timely manner after the garbage has been collected.

Do we issue notices to the offending parties, post the
offender's names on the condo bulletin board? Is maybe a
fine necessary after a certain number of offenses? Should
we assign a committee to monitor this problem and maybe
meet weekly to measure the progress?

Possible solutions were tossed around for a few minutes, and it seemed they were getting no closer to solving
the problem when my friend raised his hand.

He explained that the distance from the curb to the
side of the garage where most garbage cans resided was
probably less than ten steps. In the case of an offending
can, why not, if, as we are walking through the complex or
even driving, we could stop our car and return the can to
its rightful place? Problem solved. The neighborhood looks
were improved, a neighborly gesture was made, and we
would feel better having done our good deed for the day.

Simple solution presented by an attorney. What are the chances and at no charge?

Do You Really Need a Loan This Badly?

JW was the manager of the local office of a large bank. He had been in the banking business for many years. He started out in a small rural bank, and one of his first loans was to a young couple to buy a farm. Times were difficult, and they managed to make payments for a couple of years and then defaulted on the loan.

At that time, there was no foreclosure department in the small bank, and the duty of evicting the young couple fell upon the loan officer, JW. He enlisted the help of one of the male tellers; and they drove out to the farm, moved whatever furnishings there were out to the street, locked, and secured the property.

Although bankers are not known for having large hearts or in fact any at all, this had a lasting effect upon JW; and from that time on, he made sure that this would not happen again. He was known and often avoided by those who needed loans for fear of the interviews that he gave during the loan application process.

The bank building was laid out so that upon entering, there was a row of tellers down one side, a row of desks down the other; and at the back looking straight at the front door was JW's desk where he could keep an eye on the entire operation.

One day, a man entered the bank, and straight ahead was JW's unoccupied desk. The fellow shouted out, "JW, are you here?"

JW had been at a file cabinet at the side of his desk, and he stuck his head out the doorway and said, "Yes, yes, I am here. What can I do for you?"

The fellow then asked, "JW, have you had a bath today?"

JW was somewhat taken aback by the question and answered, "Yes, I have, and what business, may I ask, is it of yours?"

"Well, JW, I am here to see you about a loan, and I know that before I leave, I am going to have to kiss your ass, and I want to make sure it is clean."

As far as the end of the story goes, I do not know if he was granted a loan or not.

CHAPTER SIXTEEN

If You Think You Are a Person of Strong Moral
Fiber Who Can Withstand Temptation, Don't
Go to Work for a Small Town or Municipality,
or for any Government Entity for that Matter:
You May Have Misjudged Yourself.

I want to make it perfectly clear that I am not including any
problems, crimes, thefts, embarrassments, moral issues, or
just plain stupid things that our elected officials are respon-

sible for, nor am I going to give them any attaboys. Except suffice it to say they are a different breed and are the hired hands of those of you responsible for getting them elected, and so it is up to you to clean house as needed.

This is about the employees that are on the job every day, answering phones, paying bills, making excuses for the above, and in some cases, have enough time left over to figure out ways to supplement their income.

The public employees that I am calling to task are those that have found ways to gain access to the city, town, or other municipality coffers and have used them as their own checking accounts along with credit cards and other accounts and means that were at their disposal.

The public employee receives the blame when caught. However, there is also some responsibility on those who set up the systems and safeguards to prevent these abuses. I believe that in most cases, however, the person responsible for putting them in place has probably long since passed on as many of them appear that they have not been updated for at least the past hundred-or-so years.

Some people think stealing from a public entity is somehow more evil and deserves a higher penalty than from stealing from a private employer. This certainly does not apply to the Internal Revenue Service as they appear to be fair game, and even though it is technically not stealing, it is more to the point of depriving them of what they think that they are entitled to. This is probably less frowned upon and appears to be an ongoing game between the IRS and the rest of us.

I think that most employees were hired as they needed work and took it where they could find it, and there is a similar cross section of workers, be they working for a city, a state, or a private employer. I do not condone stealing from anyone, although I think it is no more of a dastardly deed to steal from a government employer than it is to steal from a private employer. As I have noted, when a person is looking for work, and a job becomes available, it usually doesn't make much difference, whether it is for a private enterprise, a government entity, a charity, or otherwise. It should also be noted that none of these have a corner on the market for honest employees.

Public entities derive their revenues from taxes that go to pay partly for basic public services. After those needs are met, the rest is rationed out to various pet projects of our elected politicians, such as making sure the Army or Air Force base in their district is kept open whether needed or not. Or funding an obsolete weapons system because the military contractor is in their district, taxpayer paid junkets to check on the price of tea in China, and other related projects.

The politician has nothing on his plate except his next election and that is the primary driver of most of their time and attention. Keeping the electorate either happy or fooled or both goes a long way in assuring him of continued access to their public trough.

The private employer, especially smaller ones, have their own money invested and must make prudent use of the funds they have to produce their product or service. A failure would hit them in the pocketbook, and their own investment would be lost.

The tax-and-spend politicians need never worry about the success or usefulness of a project. That is as long as they are perceived to be doing good work by their electorate.

With that being said, I must confess that there are good and decent politicians out there. It is just a shame that they are not more visible.

Now back to the subject at hand, which are government employees and, in particular, those of small city, town, and other municipal governments. It seems that there has been a rash of public employees caught with their hands in the public coffers as of late. Again, I must emphasize that if your moral fiber is somewhat weak, and you are trying your best to be good, you might think twice before accepting a job at a small municipality.

There is a small town nearby that a clerk mistook the town checking account for her own and began issuing checks to herself. This scheme continued over a four-year period. The amount she paid herself was almost equal to that of the town's revenue of the past year.

Where were the town officials as this was happening? Maybe they were just trying to save the taxpayer's money rather than hiring outside auditors. Did anyone ever think to check out a bank statement? I am assuming that there was probably one bank in town, and I question that someone did not at some time question some of the checks that came through rather than making sure the check had a valid signature, and there was money in the account.

I would like to have been the proverbial fly on the wall in the town council meeting when the council was notified that the bank account was getting low. I can just imagine how they must have sprung into action to figure out, which taxes could be raised to get the town solvent again.

Wondering how this could have happened so quickly, someone probably suggested calling in the clerk to see if she could add any input to what could have precipitated this problem.

Had I been part of this illustrious group, I would probably suggest making a list of the people that had access to the city cookie jar. Maybe perusing the city's bank statements of the past few months to see if any of the checks appear to be out of the ordinary. But obviously, my view of the situation through the rearview mirror provides a much clearer picture.

I suppose that the lowly clerk has been fired while the rest of the elected officials and other employees still have jobs. This is probably a good thing as this type of theft could not possibly happen on their watch again. Or could it? We would certainly hope not.

It seems as though many of these problems in other cities and town surfaced shortly after this. Could it be that other towns maybe decided that it was time they checked out how tight the lids were on their own coffers and cookie jars? I am sure that accounted for many of these problems coming to light at this time.

It appears that similar situations existed everywhere and went right up through the ranks from clerks, city managers, and department managers. The public safety departments were just as bad the others with the police and sher-iff's departments caught with their hands in the cookie jars up to their elbows.

The culprits in these schemes did not hire on with the thoughts that they were going to rip off the town. It was just too damn easy. And of course, we heard the rationaliza-tions that came from these crooks when they were caught. They included statements such as I am the only one in this place that does any work, the mayor spends most of his time having coffee with the fire chief, and the police chief spends much of his time chasing his secretary, and so on and so forth.

The following are just a few more of these schemes, versions of which can be read almost any night in your local newspaper. It does not matter whether you reside in the so-called Bible Belt of the south, the Great Mormon State of Utah in the West, a predominant Catholic or Protestant region in the northeast, or any area that somehow espouses the honesty of the local citizenry based upon the local cul-ture. There appears to be no area that is immune to or free from a little larceny from the local government employees.

It appears to be somewhat difficult to remain impar-tial when you are directing a state agency that has use of the service that a close relative provides, even if he appears to not be very competitive. Such a shame. What could we possibly do to help out this family member? In one case, it was decided to use the $1,000 threshold in which items under this amount need not have a competitive bid. The order could then be broken down to a series of smaller orders under $1,000, and the problem would be solved.

This worked out fine, but somehow, this created additional and somewhat suspicious looking paperwork along with the large number of $999 invoices to the same company, do you suppose. So bids were rigged and backdated when needed, and finally, this nepotistic company was the exclusive supplier to the department.

This type of operation taints the entire department. When the director of an agency is a crook, you can be sure that his direct underlings are aware of the problem, even to the extent of also being conspirators to the crime. They are also probably receiving perks from the director to reward them for their silence and assistance.

If you should find yourself in a similar environment, and it usually does not take long to discover what is going on, it would be wise to leave as quickly as possible. You may even want to report this as your final act before leaving. However, in many cases, it is difficult to find a responsible person that is not in on the scheme. It will though, eventually, be discovered; however, in this case, it went on for many years.

An employee at a local military base was supplementing his paycheck by selling confidential bidding information to vendors that were bidding for military contracts. The culprits in this scheme were the employee and those companies that paid him to compromise the bidding system. The employee would then have the successful crooked vendors deposit his share into offshore account.

This appeared to be a single outlaw government employee that would approach those vendors involved in the bidding process and offer them inside information for a price.

This was certainly again not rocket science by any means or a supersmart crook, but again, it is not long before those in the bidding process soon learned that to be successful at that military installation, you would need to compromise your principles. This is not unlike jumping through the hoops of third-world countries with the pay-offs and bribes needed to obtain work and favors. This type of criminal activity is difficult to detect and to uncover. It often involves only a single culprit on the government or management's side of the equation.

Another example that appears to be fairly common is that of the small government entity such as a town or small county. These usually do not need a large staff to handle the duties. A single person in some cases can be the entire staff.

It takes an ethically strong person who has the power to order and authorize purchases of supplies and services and also the authority to authorize the payment of the same, transfer monies, and so on. It is too much to ask for a person to be responsible for his own actions without the necessary checks and balances that are necessary to work in this type of environment.

This is a situation similar to one of the previous ones and netted the small-town administrator an additional income of thousands of dollars in just two years. No one should be put into this situation. We applaud the powers that be for their perceived fiscal responsibility of not spending the government entities' money, for such things as auditors and other overseers of the government piggy bank. These must not be left out of the loop that ensures fiscal responsibility. The costs associated with keeping a supposedly honest person honest are necessary and must not be overlooked.

Public entities, your money is not sacred. Your people need just as much help to stay straight as the rest of us, if that means overhauling your current policies and procedures and other standards, and it does. Do it. Spend less on travel and other expenses and hire an outside auditing firm. Be very careful of saying that the employees that you have on the payroll are either too stupid or too honest to steal as you are the one that will be proven wrong.

It was the system that created the criminal in many cases. This was unnecessary and should not have happened. There is no need to create new criminals. The jails are already overfilled. No more inmates needed, not to mention the already oversupply of dedicated crooks and criminals.

CHAPTER SEVENTEEN

The Original Crooks Begat a Smaller Copycat Crook and On and On It Goes

The perpetrators in this example appear to be some-what-less-than-innocent victims. They appeared to have almost from the beginning set out to compromise the system. There were many red flags raised during their entire operation, and no one paid any attention. Many people complained, but no one ever bothered to check anything out.

Another government entity no less. Let me make an observation that it appears some government employees just have too much time on their hands, or is this just my imagination? Please, government employees, before calling your unions, please note that the word some has been used as a qualifier. I certainly did not mean most or all.

The main characters of this scheme are a husband-and-wife team, and both were employees of the school district working together. The wife's job was purchasing books and supplies. The husband's job was writing up grant requests to the federal government. The school was entitled the grants because of a high percentage of underprivileged children that were enrolled.

I guess two wolves watching the hen house are better than one, especially if they are related.

The gist of what these nepotistic employees did in a nutshell was to make copies of textbooks, a copyright infringement, and then sold them to the school district at hyper-inflated prices through a company controlled by one of them. The result of their little scheme netted them thousands of dollars in addition to their salaries.

Next, enter the employee that worked as a secretary for the original set of crooks. She created a similar shell company and billed the school district and received payment for books never received. Supposedly, these two schemes, although very similar, were separate and both unbeknownst to the other party. This little scheme also netted her thousands of dollars also in addition to her salary. And it goes on and on.

Ah, hindsight is again wonderful as outraged district leaders ask why no one questioned the outrageous costs of the books as well as their crummy (district leaders description) quality. Thank goodness for federal grants. If the money gets low, let's apply for another. I would suppose there are also federal auditors to make sure the grant money is being wisely used, and if so, let's shift some blame to them as there is plenty to go around.

Again, the notoriety goes to the crooks. Good employees are not very newsworthy.

CHAPTER EIGHTEEN

Have I Got a Deal for You (Brother, Sister, Cousin, Friend)

If you haven't guessed by now, we are referring to the Ponzi Schemes as made famous by Mr. Madoff. He was the best at what he did, head and shoulders above most of the wannabes and pikers involved in similar schemes.

Here again, I do not believe that in the majority of cases the perpetrators of these frauds intentionally set out with criminal mischief on their minds, or to intentionally defraud anyone. There are many cases when individuals have appeared to hit the jackpot in an investment, business, or some other endeavor and assumed that it was due to their superior intellect and that they could replicate it over and over again.

The world was their oyster and luck be damned. I did it myself. I am so smart. It is also human nature that when we do accomplish something in which we are rewarded with somewhat of a financial windfall, and after all, money is the great scorekeeper, that we like to share our good fortunes with others. And more to the point, "Look at me. Aren't I great."

We not only like to share our successes with others, but we are willing to assist them in achieving their own financial success. All they have to do is turn their money over to us, and they will soon be with us on the road to easy street. When this happens, the problems begin. It is one thing to give advice and how-to lessons to the common folk, but it is another to take their money with promises of great rewards.

We now have our ego involved, we now have others depending on us for their own rewards, and we must also look and act the part of a wealthy and successful individual. Maybe a portion of the newly found investor's money can be used to keep up appearances. If a Mercedes or Lexus is a sign of success and is sufficient for most, a person as successful and smart as I am probably needs two or three, and let's not forget a boat, a vacation home, or fill in your own blank. After all, you did it once, you can do it again and again and replace the money later.

Most schemes started out this way, again, with nothing but the most honest of intentions. However, along the way, things got sidetracked. The money borrowed from the investors was not able to be replaced. Whatever it was that created the original windfall did not seem to work anymore. But it will. Be patient. You are too damn smart, and this is just a temporary speed bump, and in no time at all, you will be rolling in the chips again.

No need to go much further as I think the point has been made. But again, Mr. Ego has to be satisfied with a few more investors and some new money. You will be back on top of the world again and on and on and over and over it goes.

Now, more time is being spent recruiting new investors. You have realized by now that there is not a prayer in hell of your ever being able to recoup the losses. So now, it is the matter of keeping the little scheme afloat. Can't change your lifestyle, or folks will get suspicious. Got to keep raising new money, not only to fund your own lifestyle but to give some back to the investors for the interest and dividends that they have come to expect.

The big problem that you must now face is when people want to withdraw the fortune that you have created for them and as shown in the statements that they receive from you each month. This may be due to hard economic times, kids going to college, or just to enjoy the fruits of your brilliant investing strategy that you so generously allowed them to participate with you in.

This will eventually catch up to you, and the piper must be paid. A good run was had while it lasted, and it will end. Mr. Madoff, the poster child of Ponzi, is currently retired in a federal facility with his living expenses being paid for by Uncle Sam. Was it worth it? That is something only he can answer.

These schemes are sometimes known as affinity fraud. The general description of affinity is a relationship. Many victims have a relationship with the scheme sponsor through family members or membership in the same club or church or other organization, a well-known person in the village, or common acquaintances. When you receive a handshake, hug, clap on the back, and hear the phrase "Have I got a deal for you," it might be time to listen carefully and keep one hand on your wallet and the other on your checkbook.

I use the old saw that when the return on a proposed investment appears to be too good to be true, it probably is. However, greed is a great persuader and can soon overshadow our common sense. So if you have some spare change that you can afford to lose, then go ahead and invest (gamble). But, please, think twice before taking out a second mortgage on your home, or using you retirement account or children's college savings to fund the investment.

And in the small chance that it may be legitimate, and your relatives are all making 15 percent per month on their investment with Uncle Charlie, please forgive me if you followed my advice and missed the boat. Also, please call me and let me know where to send my check.

CHAPTER NINETEEN

Observations, Opportunities, and Advice

I must again emphasize that since we are not perfect and thank goodness for that as many auditors, law enforcement officers, jailers, lawyers, religious leaders, and advice columnists would be out of work. These folks appear to be at full employment without our unnecessarily causing additional work for them through lax rules and practices in the work place.

The events that I have noted throughout this book actually did happen. I have tried, to the best of my recollection, to report them fairly and accurately. I am sure that there are many instances of similar schemes that are ongoing. Or I may be mistaken as it appears that the culprits are usually their own worst enemies.

I would just like to offer some advice or suggestions to any of you who may find yourself in a situation that may be similar to any of those noted in the book. Do not be tempted. Report the situation to a superior. Explain your concerns that it appears that the company could be somewhat compromised if adequate controls are not put into place. And then wait to be thanked for being a conscientious and diligent employee and taking such an interest in the company. I would be very surprised if anything at all is said or done about it. In most cases, something has to be compromised before any action is taken.

However, if you have been placed in a situation that seems too good to be true, the reward easily outweighs the risk, and you have decided to go ahead and reward yourself. I might offer the following suggestions.

Make hay while the sun shines. In other words, when business is good, the company is making money, everything is good, and everyone is happy; that is the time to go for it. Do not try this when times are bad and every bit of revenue is needed, and even though it appears that no one is looking over your shoulder, they could be.

Reasonability is the watchword. It applies to your tax return as well as your little scheme. As you become more successful, and it appears that everyone in the company but you is an idiot. This is the time to be careful about increasing the frequency and the amount of your thefts, or you could screw up a good thing. When everyone around you is an idiot, be careful.

Some of us like to take vacations a time or so each year. If your little scheme has prevented you from taking a day off or, heaven forbid, a whole week or more for fear someone might discover your little scheme, someone did not think their scheme through very carefully.

And in the event that your little scheme and your case of ulcers started at about the same time, you may not be cut out for a life of crime. You might want to reevaluate the situation and start thinking about ways of extracting your hand from the cookie jar before you need a hospital stay to repair your ulcers. And remember, while you are in the hospital, there is no one back at the office covering for you.

Along a similar line as the above is the employee that becomes so wrapped up in keeping his little scheme from being found out that he has turned down promotions in order to protect himself and his scheme from being dis-covered. Hopefully, the illicit take is greater than the salary increases that would have accompanied the promotions.

My suggestion for you if you are looking for a job that offers the greatest opportunities to compromise the system would be to find a job with a small city, town, or munici-pality as they seem to offer the greatest opportunities and systems or lack thereof to be compromised. Even though, as of late, there has been a surge in the inmate population from this group. I am sure many opportunities still abound in this area.

The downside to compromising the system is being caught. A first-time offender will probably get off with a slap on the hand and might even retain his job. Each time the cookie jar is raided, it is an additional count. The more counts, the stiffer the penalties.

Whenever a person is reported to have taken a great deal of money, it is assumed that they were also probably smart enough to stash some away in an offshore or foreign bank account or elsewhere to be used later on the remote possibility of their being caught. I have only seen this in one case that I am aware of in which this was done.

The cookie jar police in most companies are somewhat vigilant, and I believe also the city, town, and other municipalities are finally coming out of the dark ages with their controls and safeguards. There will always be someone testing the system, but let us not make it so easy that we turn otherwise decent people into thieves.

CHAPTER TWENTY

Ethics, Temptations, and Obligations
of the Employer

I will comment on the first two of the above in only the broadest of terms as they are a moving target and are unique and special and apply differently to various groups and industries.

Ethics are defined as setting limits or guidelines to a range of activities that are acceptable. That behavior falling outside the range would be unacceptable. Those who find themselves involved in activities outside this range might find themselves in varying degrees of trouble. That is if they are found out.

Temptation would be defined as enticing someone to do something that is unethical for a reward of gain or pleasure.

Ethical behavior for those at the top rung of the corporate or political ladder may be somewhat different from those at the lower end. The higher the rung on which you are standing usually finds a wider range of acceptable ethical behavior. The politician as noted previously may use his position to receive perks and rewards not available at lower levels.

Top and mid management may fly first class, stay at better hotels, and charge off to expense accounts items that are not available to those who reside on the lower rungs.

Employees occupying the lower rungs of the corporate ladder have a much more narrow path of ethical behavior. They are the lowest paid and most easily replaced employees. The company has an obligation to provide work rules and safeguards to insulate them from any temptations caused by easy access to the company cookie jar.

The question that you should ask yourself prior to committing an unethical or questionable activity is, "What would my mother say if she knew what I was about to do?" We really do not need mother there because we pretty well know what she would say. This works pretty well when times are good. However, in the case of a family with financial problems, no food on the table, or in need of medical care, or other needs, the answer is not so simple. Mother will use any means available to take care of her family. This also goes for an employee with real or imagined needs.

Again, employers have an obligation to ensure that lax rules and safeguards to the company cookie jar do not encourage larceny among the employees.

CHAPTER TWENTY-ONE

A Few Closing Thoughts

I will repeat again the statement made in chapter one that the difference between those serving time and some of the rest of us is that they were caught. I have tried to note the ease in which we can be led into temptation and then into the crime by lax work rules. Most of us have never been put into a situation that we could be enriched with very little effort or risk on our part. I do not know where my threshold would be. I would hope that I will never have to find out.

I do not wish to imply that everyone is susceptible to the temptation of an easy buck with little or no risk. I am sure that there are those out there that could never be compromised. However, to be safe, it is better not to be placed into such a situation as you may find out otherwise.

I would like to relate just a short story relating to perceived values and how they apply to the real world. I have some friends who collect and restore old cars. They visit each other's collections as well as many others in the area and are often exhibiting their cars in auto shows around the West. It takes a little bit of money to pursue this hobby, and I do not believe any of them are hurting and are quite comfortable in their financial situation. I know that some of them have experienced something similar to the following.

One of my friends was exhibiting a car at an auto show when he was approached by a gentleman interested in purchasing the car that he had on display. The gentleman asked him what the price of the car would be. Well, my friend told him how difficult it had been for him to find the car and acquire it initially. He told him of the years, and the money that he had spent restoring it. The problem he had had in running down the needed parts, or having them fabricated when none were available. He summed it up with the statement that there was not enough money in the world for him to part with that car.

The gentleman disappeared for a few minutes and then returned with a check in hand and handed it to my friend. Upon seeing the check, my friend handed him the keys and said, "Thank you. You have just purchased a great car."

Throughout this book, I have tried to show how many of us have a threshold when money is involved that can change the way we think. The previous story was harmless, and no one was hurt. However, money caused a change of heart between the buyer and the seller of the car. When people say that it is not about the money, you can usually bet that it really is.

It is very easy to give the politically correct answer of absolutely and positively not to the hypothetical question of would you be tempted to take a large chunk of money if there was about a 0 percent chance of being discovered. At the time, this was probably also an honest answer. In a hypothetical situation, you cannot see the money, smell the money, or even touch it. This is a no-brainer.

However, in the real world, when the chunk is on the table before you, adrenaline flowing, heart racing, and thoughts of what it could buy, no one even aware of you and the money, things get even a little more dicey. The real world kicks in. Our threshold for honesty appears to drop considerably. What was unthinkable hypothetically appears to have some merit in the real world. Again, as I repeat for the umpteenth time, do what you must to avoid ever finding yourself in this situation.

I have reported instances in which our law enforcement officers have succumbed to the temptation of easy money. We are also not surprised when trusted people in our communities are found to be running a Ponzi scheme. We are not surprised when our elected officials are caught doing the same thing they promised to put an end to. We are not surprised when church leaders are caught with their hand in the collection plate. These and many other similar offenses are noted daily in our newspapers.

There was some point when each passed his or her threshold of "do I" or "don't I." The temptation or perceived need was so great, and the method appeared to be so easy, and the chance of being caught so remote that each of them took that first small step. And in many cases, as noted earlier, found out that it can be very addictive. And of course, it was so easy that first time, and as time went on, the frequency and amounts increased. Whatever common sense the perpetrator had at the beginning soon completely disappeared, and it was only a matter of time until the scheme was discovered.

There is some blame to go around when an employee is placed in a situation such as this. We can blame the boss or management or others for not realizing that the position had very few controls between the employee and the company wallet. The only thing that kept the employees hand out of the company wallet was the employee's own set of values. That is not good enough.

Hearken back to the headlines in the paper as noted above and add to those the story of a vice president of the United States or a governor and others that accepted payoffs and bribes, the power of money cannot be underestimated. It is easy to say what we think we would do in these instances; however, until faced with the actual situation, we really don't know for sure. Very few, it seems, are exempt from a little larceny.

The person or persons responsible for setting up the system that made it possible to be compromised will probably not be your cellmate, or even in an adjoining cell. The old boss or manager will still have his job. However, the old employee may take comfort in knowing that once caught, there will probably be some new policies, procedures, and work rules put into place that will keep it from happening again. The new employee that replaces the culprit will probably not have the same freedom or incentive to dip into the company wallet.

The rewards are not worth the risks. They include worry, health problems, heartbreak, and the embarrassment of being caught and not to mention jail time, future employment problems, and family problems. If placed into situations as I have described and no matter how easy it appears to be to supplement your paycheck, you may want to reread this book. In any case, remove yourself from the situation as quickly as possible.

CHAPTER TWENTY-TWO

Conclusion: That's All She Wrote

The events in this book actually happened. Any similarity to persons living or dead is probably not coincidental. I would suppose that these events have been repeated either in the same way, or in a closely related method many times throughout businesses everywhere, and I am sure that many are currently ongoing. Hopefully, the lid to the company cookie jars are being tightened up, plugged, and watched over just a little bit better, and there will be fewer of these problems in the future.

Let it be noted that in some cases, I have prefaced events with the statement, "As I recall." This book is based upon that statement. Some events are current, and some are somewhat older and, to the best of my knowledge and recollection, are reported as they happened.

Most of the events outlined in this book were not based upon a premeditated scheme but were conceived because of the situations into which people were placed. Please note that any reference I may have made that might in any way be construed to assume that I am condoning or offering advice on pulling off an illegal action or other stunt similar to those outlined herein was done so with tongue firmly planted in cheek.

I have, in most all cases, enjoyed my jobs and those with whom I have worked. We all run into the occasional jerk of a boss or coworker, but in my case, these have been few and far between. The years that you spend in the workplace, unless shortened by winning a lottery or coming into a large inheritance, are a substantial part of your life. Cut your losses quickly and move on. Life is too short to spend this time in an uncomfortable situation.

The thing that I find that appears to be true in so many cases is that those at the top of the corporate ladder set the pattern, attitudes, and culture for those on the lower rungs. If you do not fit in, you had better change your attitude or job because the company will not. Again, if this is an uncomfortable situation, you had better start looking elsewhere.

And when you finally find the ideal job within the ideal company. Don't screw it up because of lax work rules and policies that make it appear easy to compromise (steal). Let your feelings be known to the higher ups, make suggestions as how to correct it, or make things more secure, or in other words, police yourself. Who knows? You may even be rewarded for your efforts through promotions, raises, or bonuses. And if not, you have at least explained the weaknesses within the system, and at least, you will not be tempted.

I like to think of an acquaintance of mine that worked as a janitor for many years. He was always smiling, happy, and upbeat. Near the end of his career, one of his bosses approached him and asked how he always managed to appear so happy. He just smiled and answered that whenever he felt down or bored, he would sometimes have a drink or two during the day, and this usually perked him up and improved his attitude. He would feel better, and it was easier to get along with others, and this helped him get through the day.

The boss walked away, not knowing what to think. If his answer was true, then he had found a way to compromise the system without hurting anyone, and it did not appear to affect his work, and he was always pleasant to be around. (Please, don't try this while operating heavy equipment, automobiles, trucks, and airplanes would also be included.) If he was joking, then it was probably his way of amusing himself during a somewhat-boring career. It worked for him. Sometimes we take ourselves too seriously.

I would hope that whatever time you have devoted to this book has been enlightening, informative, and maybe even entertaining. Unlike those involved in many of the examples that, for some unfathomable reason, have pretty much lost their sense of humor and were probably neither enlightened nor entertained.

And in the off chance you are a person of impeccable character with the highest of morals, totally honest, and beyond reproach, I apologize for wasting your time as this book would appear to have no relevance to you. Especially if you have found yourself in a situation similar to any of those outlined here and withstood the temptation, I applaud you. Most of us are not so strong.

Let me end with this final comment. There are reasons why we have regulators of our financial systems, stock markets, food, health, and other industries. The free market proponents claim that the markets can and will regulate and police themselves. This is pure bunk. We have just recently recovered from one industry that almost took the entire country down. It has happened before, and it will happen again no matter how vigilant we are. Money does corrupt. Checks and balances are needed. We live in a great resilient country. We are not perfect and probably never will be, but we keep on trying.

www.ingramcontent.com/pod-product-compliance
Lightning Source LLC
Chambersburg PA
CBHW021435210526
45463CB00002B/517